Get set... GO!

New Year

Helen Bliss

Photographs by Peter Millard

Contents

About New Year	2	African drum	16
Three kings	4	Rosh Hashana apples	18
Wassail bowl	6	Chinese dragon	
Walnut boats	8	mask 1	20
Japanese fans	10	Chinese dragon	
Losar bunting	12	mask 2	22
No Ruz garden	14	Index	24

Watts Books

London • New York • Sydney

About New Year

People the world over celebrate the coming of a new year,
but not all on the same day of the year.

The activities in this book are inspired by the traditions of
people round the world on or around their New Year's da

Christians celebrate the arrival of the three kings
who brought gifts to the baby Jesus
on 6 January, called Epiphany.

It is traditional in England
to drink to everyone's good health
from the wassail bowl on New Year's Eve.

Many people then make resoluti
they try to keep in the next ye

In Japan, people hang fans around their doors
to bring them good luck for the coming year.

Buddhists celebrate New Year by painting th
homes and hanging up prayer flags, or Losar bunti

ROTHERHAM LIBRARY & INFORMATION SERVICES

This book must be returned by the date specified at the time of issue
as the DATE DUE FOR RETURN.
The loan may be extended (personally, by post or telephone) for a
further period if the book is not required by another reader, by quoting
the above number / author / title.

LIS7a

The Iranian New Year, No Ruz, falls on 20 March.
People plant little gardens a few weeks
before the date so that they bloom for the festival.

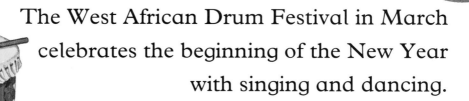

The West African Drum Festival in March
celebrates the beginning of the New Year
with singing and dancing.

The Jewish New Year, Rosh Hashana,
is celebrated in September /October.
Special foods are cooked for the family meal.

The Chinese New Year falls in February.
People dress up as dragons
and dance in the streets.
The dragon is a symbol of good luck.

> ❗ Wherever you see this sign, it means you
> should ask for help from an adult.

Three kings

Get ready

- ✔ Cardboard tubes
- ✔ Coloured paper
- ✔ Scissors
- ✔ Paints and brush
- ✔ Felt-tip pens
- ✔ Glue

...Get set

Paint the cardboard tubes bright colours.
Paint a face shape at the top.

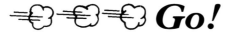 **Go!**

Cut arms, hands, beards and crowns
from coloured paper.
Glue them to the kings.
Draw eyes, mouths
and noses with felt-tips.
Decorate with stickers if you wish.

Wassail bowl

Get ready

- ✔ 2 cups apple juice
- ✔ 1 cup orange juice
- ✔ 2 cups tea (without milk)
- ✔ 1 tablespoon brown sugar
- ✔ 6 cloves
- ✔ Large bowl for serving

- ✔ 2 cups blackcurrant juice
- ✔ Half a cup lemon juice
- ✔ 1 teaspoon cinnamon
- ✔ Orange/lemon slices
- ✔ Large saucepan

...Get set

Mix the ingredients in a large saucepan.
Bring to the boil, then simmer for 15 minutes.
Remove the cloves.

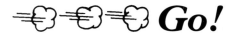 *Go!*

Decorate with slices of orange and lemon.
Serve warm from a large bowl.

Walnut boats

Get ready

✔ Small pieces of paper
✔ String
✔ Glue and Plasticine
✔ Pencil
✔ Scissors
✔ Walnut shells
✔ Matchsticks
✔ Large bowl of water

...Get set

Write New Year resolutions on the paper.
Roll them up and tie them with string.
Hang them over the edge of the bowl,
with the end of the string in the water.

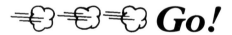 **Go!**

Cut paper sails and stick to matchsticks.
Push a lump of Plasticine into each walnut.
Stick the matchstick into it.
Give your friends a boat each.
Blow them along on the water.
See which resolution your boat sails to.

Japanese fans

Get ready

- ✔ Coloured paper
- ✔ Felt-tip pens
- ✔ Scissors
- ✔ Sticky tape
- ✔ Ruler
- ✔ Pencil

...Get set

Cut a rectangle of paper about 35 cm long.
Draw pencil lines 2 cm apart across the paper.
Decorate it with paint, pens
or shapes cut from coloured paper.

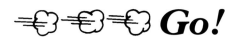 **Go!**

Fold the paper back and forth
along the lines.
Fasten one end of the fan
together with tape.
Hang it up.

Losar bunting

Get ready

✔ Crêpe paper ✔ Scissors ✔ String
✔ Stapler ✔ Pencil

...Get set

Cut some large triangles of crêpe paper.
You can cut several out at once.

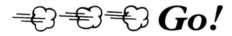 *Go!*

Fold the base of each triangle
over the string and staple it
to the other side.
Ask your friends and family to write
a wish or a prayer on each flag.
Hang the bunting up outside.

No Ruz garden

Get ready

- ✔ Medium sized bowl
- ✔ Small stones
- ✔ Small plants and bulbs
- ✔ Potting compost

...Get set

Put some potting compost into the bowl.
Carefully plant the bulbs and plants.
Press the soil down firmly.
Water the plants.

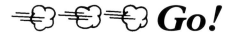 **Go!**

Create a mini garden around the plants
using the small stones.
Wait for the garden to grow!
(Don't forget to water it.)

African drum

Get ready

- ✔ Old biscuit tin
- ✔ Paint and brush
- ✔ Scissors
- ✔ Crêpe paper
- ✔ Wool and needle
- ✔ Pencil

...Get set

Paint your biscuit tin bright colours
or cover it with coloured paper shapes.
Draw around the tin on the crêpe paper.
Draw two circles wider than this one,
one 3 cm and the other 6 cm further out.
Cut out round the largest circle.
Sew large running stitches round
the middle circle line.

⇶ *Go!*

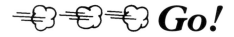

Draw the wool up so that
the crêpe paper circle fits over your drum.

Rosh Hashana apples

Get ready

- ✔ 4 medium sized apples
- ✔ 4 teaspoons raisins
- ✔ Apple corer
- ✔ Spoon and knife
- ✔ 1 tablespoon brown sugar
- ✔ 2 tablespoons margarine
- ✔ Mixing bowl
- ✔ Greased baking tray

...Get set

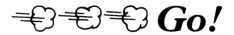

Core the apples and slit the skins all the way around the middle.

Put the apples on the baking tray.

⟿⟿⟿ *Go!*

Mix the sugar, raisins and margarine together.

Push the mixture into the apples.

Rub a little margarine on to their skins.

Bake for 45 minutes at 180°C/350°F/Gas Mark 4

Chinese dragon mask 1

Get ready

- ✔ Cardboard box
- ✔ Shoe box
- ✔ Card
- ✔ Scissors
- ✔ Newspaper
- ✔ Tape and glue

...Get set

Cut the flaps off the cardboard box.
Cut two big eye holes in the front.
Attach the shoe box to one edge
with tape like a hinge.
This makes the jaw.

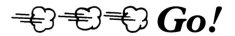 **Go!**

Cut a semi-circle of card.
Stick it above the shoe box.
Glue on scrumpled up newspaper.

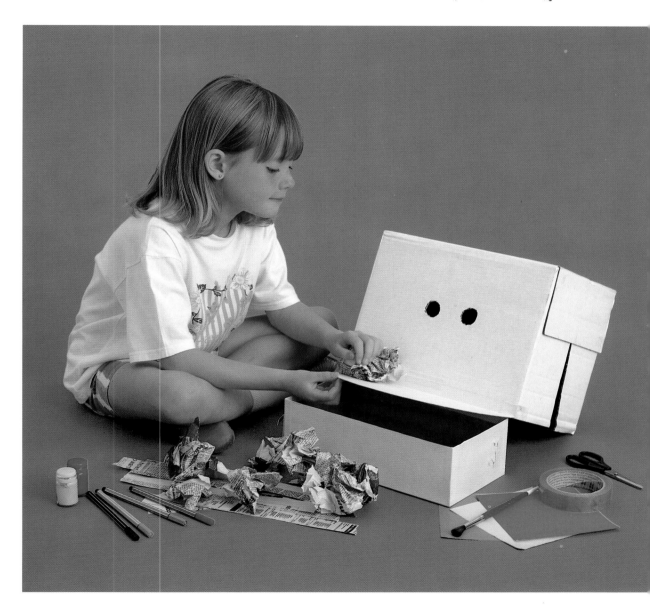

Chinese dragon mask 2

Get ready

- ✔ Base of mask (from page 20)
- ✔ Cardboard tubes
- ✔ Thin card
- ✔ Scissors
- ✔ Sticky tape
- ✔ Paint and brush
- ✔ Tinsel, crêpe paper, baubles to decorate

...Get set

Stick the cardboard tubes
on the front of the mask like nostrils.
Cut two large ears from card
and attach to the side.
Cut large white teeth and stick
inside the jaw.

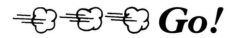 **Go!**

Paint your mask in bright colours.
Decorate with tinsel, baubles and crêpe paper.

Index

African drum 16-17

Buddhists 2

Chinese New Year 3
Chinese dragon mask
 20-23
Christians 2

dragon 3

Epiphany 2

fan 2

Japan 2
Japanese fans 2, 10-11

Losar bunting 2, 12-13

mini garden 2, 14-15

No Ruz 3, 14-15

prayer flags 2

resolutions 8-9
No Ruz 3, 14-15
Rosh Hashana 3
Rosh Hashana apples
 18-19

three kings 2, 4-5

walnut boats 8-9
wassail bowl 2, 6-7
West African Drum
 Festival 3

©1995 Watts Books

Watts Books
96 Leonard Street
London EC2A 4RH

Franklin Watts Australia
14 Mars Road
Lane Cove
NSW 2066

UK ISBN 0 7496 1528 1
10 9 8 7 6 5 4 3 2 1

Series Editor: Pippa Pollard
Editor: Sarah Ridley
Design: Ruth Levy
Cover design: Nina Kingsbury
Artwork: Cilla Eurich

A CIP catalogue record for this book
is available from the British Library

Dewey Decimal Classification 394.2

Printed in Malaysia